This journal belongs to

_____

_____

_____

Date: _____

Daily Reflections:

_____
_____
_____
_____
_____

TODAY I AM GRATEFUL FOR:

Favorite moments:

Where I can improve: _____

Tomorrow I will:

I LOOK FORWARD TO:

I challenge myself to...

Words of Affirmation:

Date: _____

Daily Reflections:

_____
_____
_____
_____
_____

TODAY I AM GRATEFUL FOR:

Favorite moments:

_____
_____
_____
_____
_____

Where I can improve: _____
_____
_____
_____
_____

Tomorrow I will:

I LOOK FORWARD TO:

I challenge myself to...

Words of Affirmation:

Date: _____

Daily Reflections:

_____
_____
_____
_____
_____

TODAY I AM GRATEFUL FOR:

Favorite moments:

_____
_____
_____
_____
_____

Where I can improve: _____
_____
_____
_____
_____

Tomorrow I will:

I LOOK FORWARD TO:

I challenge myself to...

Words
of
Affirmation:

Date: _____

Daily Reflections:

_____

_____

_____

_____

_____

TODAY I AM GRATEFUL FOR:

Favorite moments:

Where I can improve: _____

Tomorrow I will:

I LOOK FORWARD TO:

I challenge myself to...

Words of Affirmation:

Date: _____

Daily Reflections:

_____
_____
_____
_____
_____

TODAY I AM GRATEFUL FOR:

Favorite moments:

Where I can improve: _____
_____
_____
_____
_____

Tomorrow I will:

I LOOK FORWARD TO:

I challenge myself to...

Words of Affirmation:

Date: _____

Daily Reflections:

_____
_____
_____
_____
_____

TODAY I AM GRATEFUL FOR:

Favorite moments:

_____
_____
_____
_____
_____

Where I can improve: _____
_____
_____
_____
_____

Tomorrow I will:

I LOOK FORWARD TO:

I challenge myself to...

Words
of
Affirmation:

Date: _____

Daily Reflections:

_____

_____

_____

_____

_____

TODAY I AM GRATEFUL FOR:

Favorite moments:

_____

_____

_____

_____

_____

Where I can improve: _____

_____

_____

_____

_____

Tomorrow I will:

I LOOK FORWARD TO:

I challenge myself to...

Words
of
Affirmation:

Date: _____

Daily Reflections:

_____
_____
_____
_____
_____

TODAY I AM GRATEFUL FOR:

Favorite moments:

_____
_____
_____
_____
_____

Where I can improve: _____
_____
_____
_____
_____

Tomorrow I will:

I LOOK FORWARD TO:

I challenge myself to...

Words
of
Affirmation:

Date: _____

Daily Reflections:

_____
_____
_____
_____

TODAY I AM GRATEFUL FOR:

Favorite moments:

Where I can improve: _____
_____
_____
_____
_____

Tomorrow I will:

I LOOK FORWARD TO:

I challenge myself to...

Words of Affirmation:

Date: _____

Daily Reflections:

_____

_____

_____

_____

_____

TODODY I AM GRATEFUL FOR:

Favorite moments:

Where I can improve: _____

_____

_____

_____

_____

Tomorrow I will:

I LOOK FORWARD TO:

I challenge myself to...

Words
of
Affirmation:

Date: _____

Daily Reflections:

_____
_____
_____
_____
_____

TODAY I AM GRATEFUL FOR:

Favorite moments:

Where I can improve: _____
_____
_____
_____
_____

Tomorrow I will:

I LOOK FORWARD TO:

I challenge myself to...

Words of Affirmation:

Date: _____

Daily Reflections:

_____
_____
_____
_____
_____

TODAY I AM GRATEFUL FOR:

Favorite moments:

_____
_____
_____
_____
_____

Where I can improve: _____
_____
_____
_____
_____

Tomorrow I will:

I LOOK FORWARD TO:

I challenge myself to...

Words
of
Affirmation:

Date: _____

Daily Reflections:

_____

_____

_____

_____

_____

TODAY I AM GRATEFUL FOR:

Favorite moments:

Where I can improve: _____

Tomorrow I will:

I LOOK FORWARD TO:

I challenge myself to...

Words
of
Affirmation:

Date: _____

Daily Reflections:

_____

_____

_____

_____

_____

TODAY I AM GRATEFUL FOR:

Favorite moments:

Where I can improve: _____

_____

_____

_____

_____

Tomorrow I will:

I LOOK FORWARD TO:

I challenge myself to...

Words
of
Affirmation:

Date: _____

Daily Reflections:

_____
_____
_____
_____
_____

TODAY I AM GRATEFUL FOR:

Favorite moments:

Where I can improve: _____

Tomorrow I will:

I LOOK FORWARD TO:

I challenge myself to...

Words
of
Affirmation:

Date: _____

Daily Reflections:

_____
_____
_____
_____
_____

TODAY I AM GRATEFUL FOR:

Favorite moments:

_____
_____
_____
_____
_____
_____

Where I can improve: _____
_____
_____
_____
_____

Tomorrow I will:

I LOOK FORWARD TO:

I challenge myself to...

Words of Affirmation:

Date: _____

Daily Reflections:

_____
_____
_____
_____
_____

TODAY I AM GRATEFUL FOR:

Favorite moments:

_____
_____
_____
_____
_____

Where I can improve:

Tomorrow I will:

I LOOK FORWARD TO:

I challenge myself to...

Words
of
Affirmation:

Date: _____

Daily Reflections:

_____
_____
_____
_____
_____

TODAY I AM GRATEFUL FOR:

Favorite moments:

_____
_____
_____
_____
_____
_____

Where I can improve:

Tomorrow I will:

I LOOK FORWARD TO:

I challenge myself to...

Words
of
Affirmation:

Date: _____

Daily Reflections:

_____
_____
_____
_____
_____

TODAY I AM GRATEFUL FOR:

Favorite moments:

_____
_____
_____
_____
_____

Where I can improve: _____
_____
_____
_____
_____

Tomorrow I will:

I LOOK FORWARD TO:

I challenge myself to...

Words
of
Affirmation:

Date: _____

Daily Reflections:

_____
_____
_____
_____
_____

TODAY I AM GRATEFUL FOR:

Favorite moments:

Where I can improve:

Tomorrow I will:

I LOOK FORWARD TO:

I challenge myself to...

Words
of
Affirmation:

Date: _____

Daily Reflections:

_____
_____
_____
_____
_____

TODAY I AM GRATEFUL FOR:

Favorite moments:

Where I can improve: _____
_____
_____
_____
_____

Tomorrow I will:

I LOOK FORWARD TO:

I challenge myself to...

Words
of
Affirmation:

Date: _____

Daily Reflections:

_____
_____
_____
_____
_____

TODAY I AM GRATEFUL FOR:

Favorite moments:

Where I can improve: _____

Tomorrow I will:

I LOOK FORWARD TO:

I challenge myself to...

Words
of
Affirmation:

Date: _____

Daily Reflections:

_____

_____

_____

_____

_____

TODAY I AM GRATEFUL FOR:

Favorite moments:

_____

_____

_____

_____

_____

Where I can improve: _____

_____

_____

_____

_____

Tomorrow I will:

I LOOK FORWARD TO:

I challenge myself to...

Words
of
Affirmation:

Date: _____

Daily Reflections:

_____

_____

_____

_____

_____

TODAY I AM GRATEFUL FOR:

Favorite moments:

Where I can improve:

Tomorrow I will:

I LOOK FORWARD TO:

I challenge myself to...

Words
of
Affirmation:

Date: _____

Daily Reflections:

_____

_____

_____

_____

_____

TODAY I AM GRATEFUL FOR:

Favorite moments:

_____

_____

_____

_____

_____

Where I can improve: _____

_____

_____

_____

_____

Tomorrow I will:

I LOOK FORWARD TO:

I challenge myself to...

Words
of
Affirmation:

Date: _____

Daily Reflections:

_____
_____
_____
_____
_____

TODAY I AM GRATEFUL FOR:

Favorite moments:

Where I can improve:

Tomorrow I will:

I LOOK FORWARD TO:

I challenge myself to...

Words
of
Affirmation:

Date: _____

Daily Reflections:

_____
_____
_____
_____
_____

TODAY I AM GRATEFUL FOR:

Favorite moments:

_____
_____
_____
_____
_____

Where I can improve:

_____
_____
_____
_____

Tomorrow I will:

I LOOK FORWARD TO:

I challenge myself to...

Words
of
Affirmation:

Date: _____

Daily Reflections:

_____

_____

_____

_____

TODAY I AM GRATEFUL FOR:

Favorite moments:

Where I can improve:

Tomorrow I will:

I LOOK FORWARD TO:

I challenge myself to...

Words of Affirmation:

Date: _____

Daily Reflections:

_____

_____

_____

_____

_____

TODAY I AM GRATEFUL FOR:

Favorite moments:

Where I can improve:

Tomorrow I will:

I LOOK FORWARD TO:

I challenge myself to...

Words
of
Affirmation:

Date:_____

Daily Reflections:

_____

_____

_____

_____

TODAY I AM GRATEFUL FOR:

Favorite moments:

Where I can improve:

Tomorrow I will:

I LOOK FORWARD TO:

I challenge myself to...

Words
of
Affirmation:

Date: _____

Daily Reflections:

_____

_____

_____

_____

TODAY I AM GRATEFUL FOR:

Favorite moments:

_____

_____

_____

_____

_____

Where I can improve: _____

_____

_____

_____

_____

Tomorrow I will:

I LOOK FORWARD TO:

I challenge myself to...

Words of Affirmation:

Date: _____

Daily Reflections:

_____
_____
_____
_____
_____

TODAY I AM GRATEFUL FOR:

Favorite moments:

_____
_____
_____
_____
_____
_____

Where I can improve: _____
_____
_____
_____
_____

Tomorrow I will:

I LOOK FORWARD TO:

I challenge myself to...

Words of Affirmation:

Date: _____

Daily Reflections:

_____

_____

_____

_____

_____

TODAY I AM GRATEFUL FOR:

Favorite moments:

Where I can improve: _____

_____

_____

_____

_____

Tomorrow I will:

I LOOK FORWARD TO:

I challenge myself to...

Words of Affirmation:

Date: _____

Daily Reflections:

_____

_____

_____

_____

_____

TODAY I AM GRATEFUL FOR:

Favorite moments:

Where I can improve: _____

Tomorrow I will:

I LOOK FORWARD TO:

I challenge myself to...

Words of Affirmation:

Date: _____

Daily Reflections:

_____

_____

_____

_____

_____

TODAY I AM GRATEFUL FOR:

Favorite moments:

Where I can improve:

Tomorrow I will:

I LOOK FORWARD TO:

I challenge myself to...

Words
of
Affirmation:

Date: _____

Daily Reflections:

_____

_____

_____

_____

_____

TODAY I AM GRATEFUL FOR:

Favorite moments:

Where I can improve: _____

Tomorrow I will:

I LOOK FORWARD TO:

I challenge myself to...

Words
of
Affirmation:

Date: _____

Daily Reflections:

_____
_____
_____
_____
_____

TODAY I AM GRATEFUL FOR:

Favorite moments:

Where I can improve: _____

Tomorrow I will:

I LOOK FORWARD TO:

I challenge myself to...

Words
of
Affirmation:

Date: _____

Daily Reflections:

_____

_____

_____

_____

_____

TODAY I AM GRATEFUL FOR:

Favorite moments:

Where I can improve:

Tomorrow I will:

I LOOK FORWARD TO:

I challenge myself to...

Words
of
Affirmation:

Date: _____

Daily Reflections:

_____

_____

_____

_____

_____

TODAY I AM GRATEFUL FOR:

Favorite moments:

Where I can improve:

Tomorrow I will:

I LOOK FORWARD TO:

I challenge myself to...

Words of Affirmation:

Date:_____

Daily Reflections:

_____

_____

_____

_____

_____

TODODAY I AM GRATEFUL FOR:

Favorite moments:

Where I can improve:

Tomorrow I will:

I LOOK FORWARD TO:

I challenge myself to...

Words of Affirmation:

Date: _____

Daily Reflections:

_____
_____
_____
_____
_____

TODAY I AM GRATEFUL FOR:

Favorite moments:

Where I can improve: _____

Tomorrow I will:

I LOOK FORWARD TO:

I challenge myself to...

Words of Affirmation:

Date: _____

Daily Reflections:

_____

_____

_____

_____

TODAY I AM GRATEFUL FOR:

Favorite moments:

_____

_____

_____

_____

_____

Where I can improve: _____

_____

_____

_____

_____

Tomorrow I will:

I LOOK FORWARD TO:

I challenge myself to...

Words
of
Affirmation:

Date:_____

Daily Reflections:

_____
_____
_____
_____
_____

TODAY I AM GRATEFUL FOR:

Favorite moments:

Where I can improve:

Tomorrow I will:

I LOOK FORWARD TO:

I challenge myself to...

Words of Affirmation:

Date: _____

Daily Reflections:

_____
_____
_____
_____
_____

TODAY I AM GRATEFUL FOR:

Favorite moments:

_____
_____
_____
_____
_____

Where I can improve:

_____
_____
_____
_____

Tomorrow I will:

I LOOK FORWARD TO:

I challenge myself to...

Words
of
Affirmation:

Date:_____

Daily Reflections:

_____

_____

_____

_____

_____

TODAY I AM GRATEFUL FOR:

Favorite moments:

Where I can improve:

Tomorrow I will:

I LOOK FORWARD TO:

I challenge myself to...

Words
of
Affirmation:

Date:_____

Daily Reflections:

_____

_____

_____

_____

TODAY I AM GRATEFUL FOR:

Favorite moments:

Where I can improve:

Tomorrow I will:

I LOOK FORWARD TO:

I challenge myself to...

Words of Affirmation:

Date: _____

Daily Reflections:

_____

_____

_____

_____

_____

TODAY I AM GRATEFUL FOR:

Favorite moments:

Where I can improve:

Tomorrow I will:

I LOOK FORWARD TO:

I challenge myself to...

Words of Affirmation:

Date: _____

Daily Reflections:

_____

_____

_____

_____

_____

TODAY I AM GRATEFUL FOR:

Favorite moments:

Where I can improve: _____

Tomorrow I will:

I LOOK FORWARD TO:

I challenge myself to...

Words
of
Affirmation:

Date: _____

Daily Reflections:

_____
_____
_____
_____

TODAY I AM GRATEFUL FOR:

Favorite moments:

_____
_____
_____
_____
_____

Where I can improve:

Tomorrow I will:

I LOOK FORWARD TO:

I challenge myself to...

Words
of
Affirmation:

Date: _____

Daily Reflections:

_____

_____

_____

_____

_____

TODAY I AM GRATEFUL FOR:

Favorite moments:

Where I can improve: _____

Tomorrow I will:

I LOOK FORWARD TO:

I challenge myself to...

Words
of
Affirmation:

Made in the USA
Monee, IL
27 May 2021